D1357076
Right. Now this is my mother
MamAN
Does she have eyes under her fringe?
LOOK: 0/20
But actually she's a pretty cool mum.
Mum's brought me up on her own. So we're super close. But sometimes, she acts like a real kid. She gets up my nose.
I don't know my father.
PAPA
but I don't care!
Hee! Hee! I was tiny in this pic. I mean even tinier than I am now!
MY MUM'S A GAME CUBE ADDICT. Last year she gave me a Game Cube for my b'day. She's been hooked on it ever since.
OKIDOOKI!
1UP
Mum, hard at it
The worst thing is when she tries really hard to cook and it always goes wrong.
MiNA
MA MEILLEURE COPINE!
MY BEST FRIEND
MISS GRUMPY
Cool!
Elle est trop belle
Mina smiling! (very very rare)
Mina and I have been best friends since we were little. It's because I'm the only person who puts up with her bad moods! (And vice versa!)
HUHU!
The two idiots!
YO SISTA!
Jean-Pascal, her ugly dog who's got really stinky breath...
and poo.
The first time I met Mina at nursery school:
Bonk!
N
R B
Mina wants to be Missy Elliot when she grows. Sometimes she practises and I dance on stage.

JULIEN NEEL

DIARY DATES

ENGLISH TRANSLATION
BY ROS AND CHLOE SCHWARZ

First published in 2004
in the original French by
Editions Glénat
BP 177
38008 Grenoble Cedex

This English translation published
in 2007 by Usharp Comics,
an imprint of Highland Books Ltd
2 High Pines, Knoll Road
Godalming, GU7 2EP
England

Author's website: www.neelcartoons.com
ISBN-13 : 978-1-905496-10-5
Printed in France for Usharp Comics by Pollina.N° L20894C

AAAAH! HE'S TOOOO CUTE!
HAVE YOU STILL GOT A CRUSH ON THE BOY OPPOSITE?!

OH LOOK! HE'S EATING A CHICKEN SANDWICH!
WOW! SEXY.

NO ONE'S ALLOWED TO BE THAT CUTE ...
YOU'RE GOING TO HAVE TO PLUCK UP THE COURAGE TO TALK TO HIM...

TALK TO HIM?!
YES, YOU KNOW, WORDS, SENTENCES AND ALL THAT...

I DON'T FEEL QUITE READY YET...
YOU'VE BEEN SAYING THAT SINCE NURSERY SCHOOL!
AAAAH!... IT'S TIME FOR HIM TO WATER HIS BELOVED PLANT...

NOOO!

I'M HEART-BROKEN!
?

FOUILLE! FOUILLE!

* PICK, PICK!

YOU MUST BE DISTRAUGHT.
PLEASE DON'T EVER TALK TO ME ABOUT MEN AGAIN!

KNOK! KNOK!

HI. OH, IT'S YOU

WELL COME IN. YOU DON'T MIND IF I CRAWL BACK UNDER THE DUVET, DO YOU?

BOY TROUBLE.

DON'T TELL ME YOU'RE IN THAT STATE OVER A BOY YOU'VE NEVER DARED SAY A WORD TO!
THE PIG! HE PICKS HIS NOSE!

SINCE NURSERY SCHOOL I'VE BEEN IN LOVE WITH A DISGUSTING SWINE!
I WANT TO DIE!!

AND DON'T YOU EVER PICK YOUR NOSE WHEN YOU'RE ALL BY YOURSELF?

HOW DARE YOU? WHO DO YOU THINK I AM?
HEY, CHILL. IF YOU'RE GOING TO BE LIKE THAT...

THAT'S RIGHT, ABANDON ME!
SLAM!

HI, MINA? I JUST WANTED TO SAY I'M SORRY... AND ALSO, I... I THINK I'M STILL IN LOVE WITH HIM!

?

HELLO YOU!

YOU'RE A BIT SMELLY BUT YOU LOOK SWEET...

AND SOMETHING TELLS ME YOU'RE STARVING!

HEY, CHILL!
PURR! PURR!

WOW! HOW LONG IS IT SINCE YOU LAST ATE?
?
SLUG! SLUG! SLUG!

OH, WE'VE GOT A CAT NOW, HAVE WE?
LOOKS LIKE IT

I'M WARNING YOU, THERE'S NO WAY WE'RE KEEPING IT...

I HATE CATS.
WHATEVER.

PUSSY! PUSSY! PUSSY!
HEY, IT'S MY TURN!
2002. J.Neel

MORNING!
MORNING!
CIAO!
CIAO!
YAOWNN...
YAWN!
DIG! DIG! DIG!
KEBAB KING
Menu
PRESSE
GAME SOLUCE
GINO'S
CLING! CLING!
HI!
HOW'S YOUR BOOK COMING ON?
HI!
I'M WORKING FLAT OUT! DON'T ASK

Is this 15a?
Yup!

Well that's where I'm going to be living... great area!!
We can help you carry your things up if you like!

That's really nice of you! I won't say no!
No one asked you...

6th floor on the right
Oh, we're going to be neighbours!
Oh cool.

Home sweet home!

This is super precious, it's my thesis on 14th-century Italian verse!
?

Well, thanks a lot girls! I'll be having a few people round for drinks in a few days! Will you come? I've got some great organic sesame nibbles!
So that's what weighed a ton.

Perfect! He's perfect!
?
The ideal man!

The ideal man?
Are you bonkers?!! Who'd want a 30-year-old student who plays a giant violin and wears a jacket made from a dead sheep?

Hi girls! You should have come to the museum, it was BRILLIANT!
Forget what I just said
J. Nebl 2003

KNOCK! KNOCK!
?

HI! I LIVE OPPOSITE AND I WAS WONDERING IF YOU'D LIKE TO COME AND SEE A FILM...
JE...

OH! UM... YES... I... EXCUSE ME A SEC, I'VE GOT TO MAKE A PHONE CALL!
?
MUM... A NEIGHBOUR...

BIP! BIP! BIP!

HELLO?
HE'S HERE! AT MY PLACE!!!!
WHO?
HIM!

YOU MEAN... HIM???
YES, MY MOTHER'S CHATTING TO HIM IN THE SITTING ROOM! I'M TOTALLY FREAKING OUT!

RELAX! CHILL! DON'T PANIC! BE CONFIDENT!
YES, YOU'RE RIGHT...
CHIIILL

TELL YOURSELF YOU'RE STRONG! ACT COOL! YOU'RE A PRINCESS, REMEMBER! GO LOU!

RIGHT! I'M GOING! I'M HANGING UP!
GO ON. AND DON'T FORGET: YOU'RE A QUEEN!
OK, CIAO!
OK... I... I'M READY!

I'M A QUEEN, I'M A QUEEN, I'M...

AND THIS IS LOU AT 6 MONTHS, SHE WAS TEETHING. LOOK: POOR THING IT GAVE HER A HORRIBLE RASH ON HER BOTTOM!

PLEEEASE... COME OUT OF THAT TRUNK!!!!
NEVER!!!

Hi Lou!
How are you?
?
HEY!

You haven't met my mum?
I haven't had the pleasure!
Richard's just moved into the flat opposite us!

I'm having a party this evening, with a few friends... will you join us?
We'll be there!
PAF!

Gotta go! See you tonight!
BYE

He's cool, isn't he?!

HEL-LO
Anyone at ho-ome?

Right... shall we go?
I'm ready

Um... are you going dressed like that?
Why not? What's wrong with this sweater?
Haven't you got a dress?
Um... don't think so...
Come with me...

Mmm, yeah... it's ok... we've still got time... I'm sure I've got some fabric left. I'm going to fix you up something classy...
Are you sure it's worth it?
What's wrong with this sweater?

SPRING

?!

J. Neel 2003

Hi! Hi!

Hey! Hi Mina! Lou's in her room. Fancy a QUICK GAME?

Um... no thanks, don't want to disturb you...
DIG! DIG!

Take THAT, Doctor Robotix!!!
WOW

Don't you think we should do SOMETHING about your mother? She's turning into a couch potato...
You're telling me...

Gotta find her a boyfriend: she's been glued to the GameCube for the last three weeks!

What about your neighbour Richard? Can't we get them together?

She's got to get off the sofa first!

Hey, isn't that THE FUSE BOX for all the apartments in your block?
?

Um... yeah, it is... so what?
Duh! Think!

Oh yes!!! It could work!!!
And a love affair begins!!!
CHTIC!

Richard! Have you got a power cut too??!!

* DRIVING SCHOOL

SOAP

SPO!!

DIG!
DIG!
DIG!
DIG!
DIG!
DIG!

BREK
KO!
PLAYER 1 WIN !

YESSS!
THAT'S IT, YOU WON!
NEXT TIME WE'LL PLAY CHESS...

SOAP

OH, HI! UM... YOU...
OH, HELLO, I...
SO YOU TOO, YOU...
YOU TOO, YOU...
YES.
IN THE LAUNDRY TO...

IT'S UM... REALLY CONVENIENT...
...FOR DOING THE...
YES. HA! HA!
WASHING?
YES, THE WASHING.
HA! HA!
!

WELL... UM... I...
UM... DO FANCY GOING TO SEE A FILM ONE EVENING?
OH YES!... YES
WE...
G... GREAT
YES.
CIAO!

?
WHAT THE...?!
BUT... BUT!!! OH NO!

MUM, DON'T BE CHILDISH, COME OUT OF THERE...
NEVER!!

ARE YOU SURE YOU REALLY NEEDED ME TO COME WITH YOU?
MARCHÉ BIO
YOU'VE GOT TO GET OUT FROM TIME TO TIME!
VOLAILLES
ANYWAY, ISN'T IT GREAT WANDERING AROUND LOOKING AT ALL THIS BEAUTIFUL NATURAL FOOD THAT...

HEY!
RICHARD
HOW'S IT GOING?
GREAT! I HAD A JOB GETTING LOU TO COME TO THE MARKET WITH ME, IT'S GOOD FOR HER...

BESIDES, I LOVE WANDERING AROUND LOOKING AT ALL THIS BEAUTIFUL NATURAL FOOD THAT...

PRIM

?
RICHARD

ISSON

DID YOU SEE THE WAY HE WAS LOOKING AT THAT GIRL ON THE FISH STALL?

?

SO WHAT? ARE YOU JEALOUS OR WHAT?

WHAT? ME, JEALOUS? HUH!
NO WAY! HUH!
WHAT RUBBISH!

WELL, ACTUALLY, I AM...
WHAT?
I THINK I AM A TINY BIT JEALOUS!

SO THAT MEANS THAT YOU'RE IN LOVE WITH HIM THEN?
DO YOU THINK?

Sidera, the space warrior had just landed on the planet Oceanus, where the devious Neptuna was holding Prince Falgor captive…

No sooner had she entered the coral fortress than an army of the witch's crabmen attacked her from all sides…

Experienced in the art of galactic combat, Sidera had no difficulty in overcoming the guards and reaching the room where the terrifying mer-woman was holding the handsome Prince Falgor prisoner…

But, with a cunning magic trick, Neptuna disarmed the brave defender of galactic justice…

"This time you're done for, Sidera. The prince is in my power!" sniggered the enchantress.

Quick as a flash, Sidera floored the evil creature with a powerful high kick to the jaw.

"That'll teach you, bitch!" retorted our heroine as the witch of the deep lay on the ground, revealing her disgusting thighs pockmarked with cellulite.

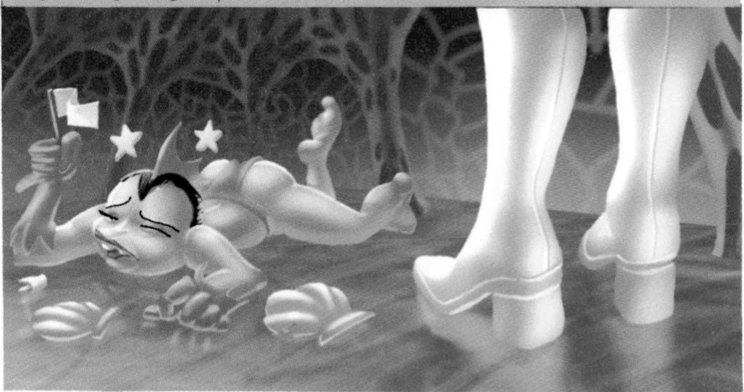

"Fear not, your highness! I have come to free you from the clutches of this witch!" announced the statuesque she-warrior, snapping the prisoner's chains.

"Sidera, you have saved my life," murmured the prince. "How can I thank you?"

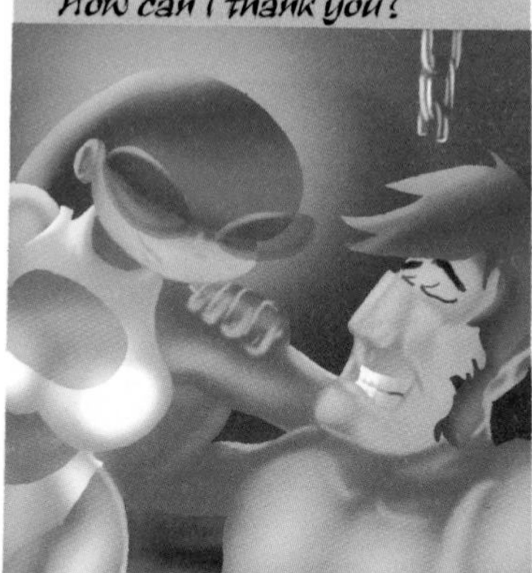

UM... I'VE JUST HAD YOUR HEADTEACHER ON THE PHONE. APPARENTLY YOUR P.E. TEACHER'S NEVER SET EYES ON YOU...
UH OH!

OK, I PLEAD GUILTY! BUT I'VE GOT MITIGATING CIRCUMSTANCES!
IT MUST BE UNDER HERE...

AH! HERE IT IS. IT'S BAD ENOUGH BEING MADE TO WEAR A TRACK SUIT... YUCK! LOOK AT THAT, IT'S LIMP, SHAPELESS, THE COLOURS ARE VILE....
...AND BESIDES, I DON'T PARTICULARLY LIKE THE SMELL OF PERSPIRATION...

...ESPECIALLY AT 10 AM, JUST AFTER BREAKFAST! I'M BARELY OUT OF BED AND I'M BEING FORCED TO DRESS UP LIKE A RAPPER IN A CHANGING ROOM THAT STINKS OF ROTTING FLESH...

BUT YOU KNOW THAT PHYSICAL EXERCISE IS VERY IMPORTANT! YOU HAVE TO LEARN TO DISCIPLINE YOUR BODY! PLATO WROTE SOME VERY INTERESTING THINGS ON THE SUBJECT...
...AND BESIDES:
?

WE'RE GOING FOR A JOG IN THE PARK RIGHT NOW! FRESH AIR?!

WELL? DON'T YOU FEEL GREAT? CAN'T YOU JUST FEEL YOUR LUNGS FILLING WITH FRESH AIR?!
YEAH, RIGHT...
IF ANYONE SEES ME, THAT'S THE END OF MY SOCIAL LIFE...

AND... COUGH... AS THE PHILOSOPHER...COUGH... SAYS...
COUGH! COUGH!!
ARGH! I'VE GOT A STITCH.
IS THAT WHAT THE PHILOSOPHER SAYS?

NO, SILLY! HE SAYS: "A HEALTHY MIND IN—COUGH! COUGH!... IN LATIN 'MENS SANA IN CORPORE SANAAAGH!'
KREUU! OWARGL! TOUSS!
NO WONDER LATIN'S A DEAD LANGUAGE...

RIGHT! MY MISTAKE: YOU WERE RIGHT. SPORT'S GREAT, I'M ON WICKED FORM...
HOP! HOP!
SHALL WE DO THIS AGAIN TOMORROW?

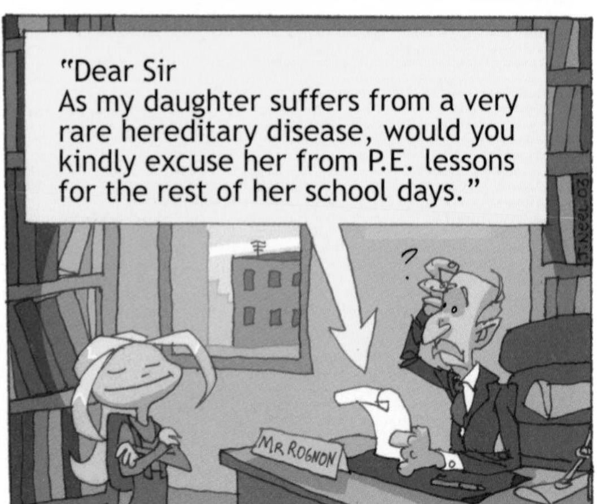
"Dear Sir
As my daughter suffers from a very rare hereditary disease, would you kindly excuse her from P.E. lessons for the rest of her school days."
?
MR ROGNON

?
?

GIN

AFX

J. NOEL 2008.

I'VE GOT HIS MOBILE NUMBER!
?

YEAH, BUT I'VE NEVER DARED CALL HIM...

A TEXT? YES! YOU'RE RIGHT!
?

SO, UM... "I LOVE YOU"... NO. TOO DIRECT. "YOU'RE TOO GORGEOUS"... NO GOOD: HE'LL THINK I'M SHALLOW...

"I LOVE YOUR INTELLIGENCE". THAT'S GOOD! AND IT'S FLATTERING...

I.L.O.V.E. Y.O.U.R. I.N.T.E.L.... AAGH! IT'S TOO LOOONG! IT DOESN'T FIT!!
BIP! BIP! BIP!

GOT TO FIND SOMETHING SHORTER...

I LOVE YOUR WIT!

THAT'S PERFECT!
RIGHT:
I. L.O.V.E. Y.O.U.R...
BIP! BIP! BIP!

!?
BIP!

AAAGH! STUPID CAT!!! YOU PRESSED SEND AND I HADN'T FINISHED!!!

I LOVE YOUR WI....

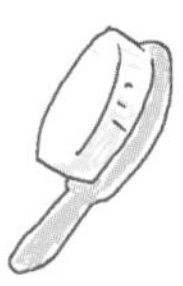

Knock! Knock! Knock!
Oh! Who's there?

It's me, from next door!
Wow! You look just like me!
Amaaaazing!

What shall we do now? Shall we do our hair?
Or we can try on clothes???

Or we could go in the swimming pool!
Yes! Anyway this hairbrush is much too big!

This is fun, isn't it?
Maybe it needs water!

Oh! Here's my husband on his horse!
Clipclop! Clipclop!
Yo

Hey! Your husband's dressed like Prince Charming!
Poor thing, he hasn't got any other clothes...
And my hair's made of plastic...

Right, what shall we do now?
Shall we do our hair?
Or we can try on clothes?
Well I'm going off for a ride.

...

We've got to face facts: we're too old to play with dolls.
Yeah.. all the magic's gone...

* CHAMBER OF HORRORS

HEY, IT'S HALLOWEEN, COME ON, LET'S TELL GHOST STORIES!
WHAT? BUT I'VE GOT LOADS OF HOMEWORK AND...
I'LL WRITE YOU A NOTE!

LOOK! I'VE BOUGHT LOADS OF GROSS SWEETS FOR OUR SPOOKY EVENING.
HERE WE GO AGAIN...

THEY SAY THAT ON A CERTAIN ROAD, WHEN THERE'S A FULL MOON, YOU MIGHT MEET A STRANGE GIRL HITCH-HIKER DRESSED IN WHITE...
HEEELP...

...AND AFTER A FEW MILES, SHE VANISHES, BECAUSE ACTUALLY, SHE'S A GHOST WHO'S COME BACK TO HAUNT THE PLACE WHERE SHE WAS KILLED.
OH. YOU KNOW IT?

AND THE COUPLE WHOSE CAR BREAKS DOWN IN THE FOREST? THEY HEAR A NEWS FLASH ON THE RADIO...
...SAYING A DANGEROUS MADMAN WITH A HOOK HAS ESCAPED FROM A NEARBY ASYLUM ETC. ETC....
EVERY-BODY KNOWS THAT ONE.

RIGHT, I'M GOING TO BED. I'VE HAD ENOUGH OF YOUR STORIES.
AND THE ONE ABOUT THE BLOODY HAND THAT...

OK, BEDDYBYES...
YAAAWN

RAAAAAAHH!
A BEAST! THERE'S A BEAST IN MY BED!

OH IT'S THE CAT... IT'S YOU... I... I KNEW IT! GOT YOU!
HEHEH!
CLIC!
G..GOOD NIGHT...
?

GRIIIIIIIKT!
IT'S FUNNY, ALL THE NOISES YOU HEAR AT NIGHT IN OLD BUILDINGS...
TUD!
IT'S ALL VERY WELL SAYING IT'S THE WOOD CREAKING AND THE PIPES GURGLING...
GUDUGDUG!
SSSSSKTT...

FFWOOOOOO...
KRRIIIRKA!
KLIKTONG!
JUNK!

OK, YOU CAN SLEEP IN MY BED AGAIN THIS YEAR, BUT THIS IS THE LAST TIME!
THE WHITE LADY AND THE MADMAN WITH A HOOK... THEY'RE COMING TO GET ME...
J.Neel 2003

OOOH! MY LITTLE PRINCESS HAS WOKEN UP AT LAST! I'VE MADE YOU ORANGE BLOSSOM FLAVOURED PANCAKES!
?

I'VE IRONED THE PRETTY DRESS I MADE YOU FOR YOUR COMMUNION!
THE PINK ONE, YOUR FAVOURITE!

SEE YOU THIS EVENING MY FAIR-HAIRED ANGEL!

BABY! MUMMY'S BROUGHT YOU YOUR TEA!

AS YOU'VE BEEN SUCH A POPPET, I'VE BOUGHT YOU A RAINBOW PONY FOR YOUR COLLECTION!
OH, YOU'RE ALL GRUBBY, MY PRECIOUS! HOLD ON, I'VE GOT A HANKY!

GUESS WHAT? ON SATURDAY WE'RE GOING TO SEE CÉLINE DION LIVE!
THE TWO OF US!
A GIRLS NIGHT OUT.

SUGARPLUM, LET ME INTRODUCE THE CHAIR OF THE MINI-MISS JUDGES. SHE'S COME TO SEE YOUR LITTLE DANCE ROUTINE.
HELLO LITTLE TREASUUURE!
GNUP GNUP

WHAT A DAAAARLING!
AND YOU KNOW, SHE'S ALSO TOP OF HER SILKSCREEN PAINTING CLASS!

RAAAAAAHH!

A NIGHTMARE! IT WAS A HORRIBLE NIGHTMARE!

HI LOULOU! YOU HAVEN'T SEEN THE PAPER WITH THE CHEATS TO THE VIDEO GAMES IN, HAVE YOU?

?

BIP!
BIP!

BRRBRRRBRRBRRR
?

EXCUSE ME, MISS, DON'T YOU THINK YOU'RE A BIT LATE?

WHAT? OH, IT'S YOU! CHILL, I'M READY! I'LL BE DOWN IN TWO TICKS!

MATH

STADAAM!♪

?
MINA?

I DON'T BELIEVE IT! SHE DIDN'T WAIT! AND SHE CALLS HERSELF MY FRIEND!

I HATE YOU!
J.NeeL.02

THIS TIME...
CUISINE FACILE

S.INE CILE

SHALL WE GO?

HI GINO!
CIAO BELLA! YOUR TABLE'S READY, GIRLS!

JOUETS
WHAT'S UP WITH YOU? DON'T YOU LIKE CHRISTMAS OR WHAT?

WELL, MY PARENTS HAVE JUST GOT DIVORCED, YOU KNOW, AND IT'S WEIRD TO BE SPENDING CHRISTMAS WITHOUT MY DAD THIS YEAR...
YEAH, THAT'S A BUMMER.

I... I'M SORRY... I
WHAT? SORRY FOR WHAT?

WELL, UM... YOU... YOU DON'T KNOW YOUR DAD AND...
HA, HA! NO PROB...

AS I HARDLY KNOW HIM, I DON'T MISS HIM!

BUT UM... HOW... Y'KNOW?
HOW DID IT HAPPEN?

YOU DON'T MIND...
...TALKING ABOUT IT? NOT AT ALL!
QUITE THE OPPOSITE!

LET'S MAKE SOME HOT CHOCOLATE AND I'LL TELL YOU THE WHOLE STORY.

So...

When she was a teenager, Mum was, how can I put it... a bit wild ...

And she had quite a lot of rows with my Grandma and Grandpa...

When she met my dad at a party, it was love at first sight, and she didn't stop to think...

They moved into a little studio flat in the centre of town and were madly in love for a few months...

Then one day, Mum did a pregnancy test...

But he wasn't at all ready to have a kid...

It was really hard, but they decided to split up...

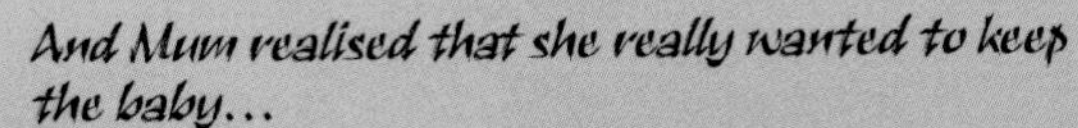
And Mum realised that she really wanted to keep the baby...

Luckily.

At first it wasn't easy for her to look after me and carry on studying...

...and working part-time...

But we coped, and things turned out fine!

THERE!

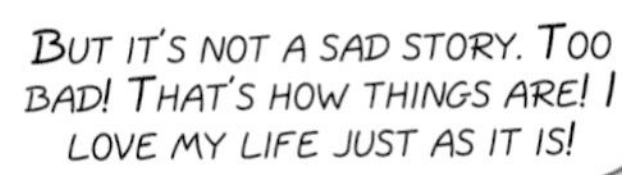
BUT IT'S NOT A SAD STORY. TOO BAD! THAT'S HOW THINGS ARE! I LOVE MY LIFE JUST AS IT IS!

YES, YOU'RE PROBABLY RIGHT....

I SUPPOSE THERE'S NO POINT REGRETTING THE PAST...
YEAH. AS THE PHILOSOPHER SAYS: "THE SHOW MUST GO ON"!

ANYWAY, YOU'LL GET TWICE AS MANY PRESENTS NOW!
THAT'S TRUE!
HAPPY CHRISTMAS LOULOU!
HAPPY CHRISTMAS MINA!

IT'S NO GOOD, HE DOESN'T WANT TO WEAR HIS LITTLE HAT!
PRESSIES! PRESSIES!

A COOKBOOK! HEE! HEE! IS THAT A HINT?
LA CUISINE FACILE

A LAPTOP???!? THAT'S... THAT'S AMAAAZING!

HAPPY CHRISTMAS MUM, YOU'RE A STAR

I LOVE YOU VERY MUCH, YOU KNOW...
I KNOW.

DARLING? COME AND OPEN YOUR PRESENT!

COMING.

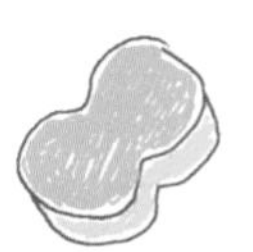

?
BEEP-BRRR-BEEP

HELLO? OH MUM, HI. I... WH... WHAT? AT THE STATION? BUT?! AND UM... A TAXI? OH BUT WE... WHAT? HELLO? HELLO?

PANIC STATIONS!
GRANDMA'LL BE HERE IN TWENTY MINUTES!!!

WHEW
TAP! TAP!

MUM!
GRANDMA!

THIS PLACE IS A TIP, AS USUAL!
CHILL!

WHAT'S THIS DISGUSTING CREATURE?
UM. THAT'S MY LITTLE KITTEN

HE'S VERY UGLY.
AND HE STINKS.

DID YOU REALLY NEED TO SADDLE YOURSELVES WITH THIS ANIMAL?
THIS TEA'S VILE.

I KNEW IT! YOUR FRIDGE IS FULL OF AMERICAN JUNK FOOD!
AND YOU HAVEN'T EVEN GOT ANY BRUSSELS SPROUTS!
RIGHT, I'M GOING OUT TO BUY SOME FOOD.

AND YOU'RE COMING WITH ME! THERE'S NO WAY I'M GOING OUT ALONE IN THIS CITY TEEMING WITH DELINQUENTS...
OOOW!

HI!
UH-OH
?

MUM, LET ME INTRODUCE RICHARD, A NEIGHBOUR WHO, UM... I MEAN A FRIEND WHO I... I MEAN WHO... A NEIGHBOUR.
HOW DO YOU DO?

THIS ONE TOO: HE'S UGLY AND SMELLY

RICHARD, PLEASE
HUMPH HIPPY, DRUG ADDICT NOT OUR TYPE

SO, UM, HOW LONG DO YOU PLAN TO STAY?
ONE WEEK

BLINK

WHAT ON EARTH HAPPENED TO YOU?
HMM. YOUR MOTHER MADE A SPECTACLE OF HERSELF IN PUBLIC AS USUAL!

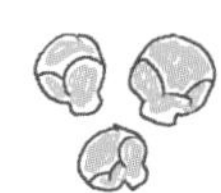

WELL, WE'RE OFF. SEE YOU LATER. WE'RE LEAVING YOU IN CHARGE.
HAVE A GOOD DAY, GRANDMA!

SLAM!
YES, THAT'S RIGHT, LEAVE ME ALL ALONE LIKE A SAD OLD WOMAN...

WHEN YOU COME BACK, WITH A BIT OF LUCK YOU'LL FIND ME DEAD!
TWO DAYS, TWO DAYS TILL SHE LEAVES...
HANG IN THERE...

?
Zz

Zz

WOOF
NKFFF!

SNIGGER, SNIGGER!

COME ON, BE STRONG. WE'VE GOT TO GO HOME NOW.

SNIFF! SNIFF? OH HEAVENS! CAN YOU SMELL THAT?
BRUSSELS SPROUTS...
AGAIN...
YEURK.

PUSSY! PUSSY! PUSSY!

AHEM
?

HMM. I WAS MAKING SURE YOUR MONSTER ISN'T FLEA-RIDDEN...
YEAH, YEAH...

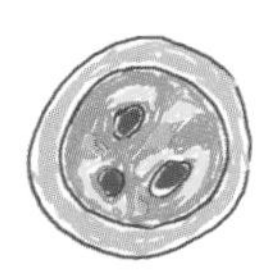

Come on, let's take a souvenir photo of your visit!
Clic!
BZZZZ

This is ridiculous! You'll make me miss my train with your nonsense!
Cheeese!
Cheeeeeeese!
FLASH!

Aaaagh! Give that to me, you imbecile!
TAXI

Goodbye Grandma!
It's a waste of time, she's not even looking at us...

Wahay! Pizza tonight!
Yay! No more Brussels sprouts!

?
ZIFT!

A VALENTINE'S CARD!!!

?
IT'S FOR ME!

HOW DO YOU KNOW?
MAYBE IT'S FOR ME!
GIIIIIIVE IT!
MIIINE!

MAYBE IT'S FROM RICHARD?
NO, OUCH!
I BET IT'S FROM TRISTAN!

RICHARD!

TRISTAN!!
CATCH!

RICHARD!!!

YOU WON. YOU READ IT FIRST.

WELL...

ARE YOU IN LOVE? IN LOVE WITH PRIME-QUALITY MEAT? WELL YOU'LL BE SWEPT OFF YOUR FEET BY OUR SPECIAL OFFER ON PORK ROASTS AT YOUR LOCAL AWARD-WINNING BUTCHER'S TODAY!

DITES LUI AVEC DES FLEURS
ST-VALENTIN

14 Fevrier:
UN CADEAU DE LA TAILLE DE VOTRE AMOUR!

FÊTE DES AMOUREUX PRIX DE GROS SUR L'ÉLECTROMÉNAGER
POISSONNERIE
PROMO! LE HARENG, LE POISSON DE L'AMOUR -50%
POISSON PASSION

HIYA!
OH HI

WOW! WHAT'S UP WITH YOU?
NOTHING. I'M SICK OF ALL THIS IN-YOUR-FACE LOVEY-DOVEY STUFF

VALENTINE'S DAY? SO DIDN'T TRISTAN SEND YOU A VALENTINE'S CARD?
HUH. NO. THANK GOODNESS. THAT'D BE SOO CHEESY!

ANYWAY, I THINK IT'S REALLY COOL HE'S NOT A SUCKER FOR ALL THAT STUPID ROMANTIC RUBBISH...

MEAN — HAVEN'T YOU SEEN THE ADS? LOVE, LOVE, LOVE — TO MAKE PEOPLE BUY ALL SORTS OF CRAP!

VALENTINE'S DAY MY A...
AHEM... UM... LOU?

I UM... I MEAN I WANTED TO GIVE YOU THIS AND ASK YOU TO... I MEAN YOU'LL SEE...
IT'S ALL WRITTEN INSIDE...
AND UM...

WELL, UM... SEE YA...!

DON'T SAY A WORD OR I'LL NEVER TALK TO YOU AGAIN...
UM... ACTUALLY I WAS THINKING OF A LOUD SNIGGER...

HEY! GUESS WHAT?!? I'VE GOT A VALENTINE'S CARD!
SO HAVE I!!!
LET'S DANCE!
WAHAY!!
CLIC!
BOUM TCHIKA BOUM TCHIK
BOUM TCHIKA
BOUM TCHIK
BOUM TCHIKA
BOUM!
LOVE DOESN'T HALF MAKE YOU STUPID...
YEAH. BUT IT'S SOOO GOOD!

©BOULET

Knock! Knock!
Here they are!
Hold on a sec, I'll just finish my game...

Umm... Boo!
Hey, guys!

Mwah!
Let me just save it and then I'm all yours!

Oh!
Wow! Soul Calibur 3!!
Yeh! It's just out, I bought it this afternoon!
Who's jealous?

Can I have a go?
Sure!

Look, if you press A and B, you rip out his spine!!!
Wicked!

Um... we'd better get a move on... the restaurant...
Cool! His brain's coming out of his nose!

Why don't we order pizza instead?
But...
Four cheeses for me.

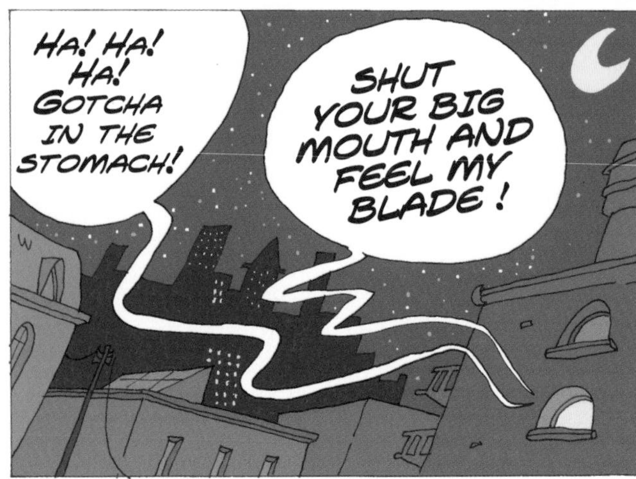
Ha! Ha! Ha! Gotcha in the stomach!
Shut your big mouth and feel my blade!

It's weird but I had a very different idea of a romantic evening.
Yes, me too.
I'm going to spill your guts!
Swallow your teeth, filthy dog!
Pizza
Pizza
Pizza

Right, time for me to go.
Me too, it's late, my dad'll kill me!
Pow! Meanwhile, I'm the one who's killed you!
PIZZA
PIZZA

Come back anytime you like to get your revenge!
'Bye girls!!!
Good night Richard.
You're on!!!

Aaah! What a great evening! We had a ball, didn't we?
No!

No?
No.

What's your problem?
Has it occurred to you that you ruined Valentine's Day?
PIZZA

Valentine's Day... Oh no... I completely forgot...
Forgot? I don't believe it! The night the guys finally get round to declaring their love, and you FORGOT?!

No, but I...
I don't know what got into...
It's that game...
See you in the morning.

From: Lou To: Tristan
Subject: Hi!
Just a quick email while I'm having breakfast to give you a kiss! Ciao xxx Lou :o)

TRISTAN! COOOL! DID YOU GET MY EMAIL? HEE! HEE! HEY, I MUST TELL YOU ABOUT MY MUM'S LATEST...
NOW WHAT'S SHE DONE?

IN THE CAT TRAY! YESSS! I PROMISE! GOTTA GO, WE'RE AT SCHOOL NOW! WE'LL TEXT, OK? BYE!
BYE!

fm: Lou to: Tristan wot r u doing?
fm: Tristan to: Lou im in class
fm: Lou to: Tristan me 2 im bored
fm: Lou to: Tristan me 2

fm: Lou to: Tristan doin smth 2nite?
fm: Tristan to: Lou nothin spesh

fm: Lou to: Tristan c u at park?
fm: Tristan to: Lou wot time?
fm: Lou to: Tristan 6?
fm: Tristan to: Lou cool

I'm writing you a note while the rest of the class is doing P.E. Cellphone can't get a signal in the library. Boring, boring. I'll pass this to you later.

HELLO? YEAH, IT'S ME! I'M ON THE BUS. BE THERE IN A MINUTE. HOW WAS YOUR DAY?
YEAH, COOL. AND YOURS?

... AND OUR TEACHER WAS REEALLY HARSH. WE WERE WELL ANNOYED...
YEAH, BUMMER

I'M AT THE PARK!
ME TOO!
WHERE ARE YOU?
IN FRONT OF THE KIOSK.
OH YES, I CAN SEE YOU!

HI
HI!
CLAP!
BIP!

25
MAI

GOOD MORNING DAAARLING! IT'S MUMMEEE! I'VE BROUGHT YOU BREAKFAST IN BED!
BUT IT'S 5 O'CLOCK IN THE MORNING AND IT'S SATURDAAAY...

OH YES, DRAT: IT'S SATURDAY 24TH MAY. BAH!
BUT STILL, A SPONTANEOUS TREAT IS NICE, ISN'T IT?

OOOOOH! WHAT A BRILLIANT CATALOGUE! IT'S FULL OF EXCITING THINGS! LIKE THIS CHINESE TEA SET AND THIS BOXED SET OF BUFFY SEASON 3 DVDS, AND EVEN... OH WOW: THE NEW SUPER MARIO FOR THE GAMECUBE!
...AND THEY'RE VERY REASONABLY PRICED!!
ORANGE JUICE
GIFTS

OH YES! THAT? IT'S A CALENDAR I BOUGHT SO I WOULDN'T FORGET IMPORTANT DATES.
?
SAMEDI
24
MAI

BY THE WAY, TOMORROW, WILL YOU REMIND ME TO CALL GRANDMA TO WISH HER SOMETHING!
EH... OK... I'M GOING OUT, I'M MEETING MINA!.
CIAO!

HERE, I'LL GIVE YOU SOME MONEY, I DUNNO, JUST IN CASE YOU WANT TO BUY SOMETHING.
CLIGNE! CLIGNE!*

*wink wink

SEE YOU TONIGHT, DAUGHTER!

HEY
HEY!

BY THE WAY, YOU KNOW IT'S MOTHER'S DAY TOMORROW, DON'T YOU?
I THINK I'VE GOT THE MESSAGE.

LISTEN TO THIS. I'VE JUST THOUGHT OF A BRILLIANT IDEA FOR BREAKING THE ICE BETWEEN MY MUM AND RICHARD!
HMM?
YEAH. THEY'RE LIKE KIDS. NEITHER OF THEM DARES MAKE THE FIRST MOVE.

I RENT A REALLY SLUSHY DVD, TITANIC OR SOMETHING, AND I INVITE RICHARD TO COME OVER AND WATCH IT...

... AND IN THE MIDDLE OF THE FILM, I SAY LIKE I'M KNACKERED AND I LEAVE THE PAIR OF THEM IN AN OCEAN OF SLUSH!
BRILL!
WILL YOU CALL ME?

YAAWN! I'M WIPED, I'M OFF TO BED. NIGHT!
AREN'T YOU DYING TO FIND OUT IF THEY ESCAPE THE ICEBERG?

HELLO MINA? OPERATION SARDINE'S GOING ACCORDING TO PLAN! TIME FOR PHASE 2.
JACK!
AU SEGLOUB!

THAT'S IT, THE FILM'S OVER, THEIR EYES ARE BRIMMING WITH TEARS!
NOW THEY SHOULD RISE TO THE BAIT!

AND AiiiiEiiiAiii WILL ALWAYS LOOOOVE YOUHOUWOUHOUWOU!
SNIFF!
SOB

GREAT FILM
YES
MOVING LOVE STORY
FAB COSTUMES
THE ICEBERGS...
AMAZING SPECIAL FX.
SO MANY DIED
AND IT'S ROMANTIC!
I AGREE

ARE YOU THINKING WHAT I'M THINKING?

AHA! I THINK THEY'RE READY TO TAKE THE PLUNGE!

CANCEL THAT. MY PLAN'S A WASH-OUT...

A-9!
AIRCRAFT CARRIER SUNK!

OH NO, I'M SKINT! I HAVEN'T GOT ANY DOSH TO BUY TRISTAN A BIRTHDAY PRESENT!
?

HERE'S A GREAT IDEA. WHY DON'T YOU WALK OLD LADIES' DOGS IT'S EASY AND THE OLD DEARS ARE TOO ARTHRITIC TO COUNT OUT LOOSE CHANGE SO THEY'LL GIVE YOU A NOTE.
OH YEAH...

COME ON BABY, YOU'RE GOING WALKIES WITH THIS NICE LITTLE GIRL...
AND MAMMA'S GOING TO WATCH THE YOUNG AND THE ....

....RESTLESS

?
TRAVAUX

PAF!

WAF! WAF!

HELLO PRECIOUS! HAPPY TO BE HOME WITH MAMMA?
LET'S GIVE THE LITTLE GIRL FIVE EUROS TO SAY THANK YOU!

A BOTTLE OF ANTISEPTIC, A PACK OF DRESSINGS, BLISTER CREAM AND A BIG ROLL OF SURGICAL TAPE...
THAT'LL BE EXACTLY FOUR EUROS!

EXPRESSION ARTISTIQUE
OK CLASS. NOW'S THE MOMENT TO SHOW YOUR WORK. REMEMBER, THE PROJECT IS: EXPRESS YOUR DOUBTS AND ANXIETIES ABOUT THE FUTURE THROUGH A WORK OF ART; A DRAWING, A SONG, ANYTHING YOU LIKE!

WELL, I'VE DONE A COLLAGE WITH PHOTOS OF MY FAVOURITE ACTORS! GEORGE'S FOREHEAD, LEONARDO'S EYES AND BRAD'S CHIN!
THIS IS MY "PRINCE CHARMING". HEE! HEE! HEE!

THIS IS A YOGHURT-POT SCULPTURE. IT REPRESENTS THE OFFICES OF THE MULTINATIONAL COMPANY THAT I HOPE TO RUN WHEN I'M OLDER.

THIS PAINTING SHOWS US THAT SOMETIMES PEOPLE CAUSE POLLUTION AND THAT'S BAD BECAUSE IT MAKES THE PLANET SICK...

YO! YO! SISTA! HEY, YO, I PICK UP THE MIC TO CALL ON THE SISTAS TO BE HOW YOU LIKE YEAH! COS WE THE RASTAS!
POUM TOU POUM TOUM TCHAC!
CHECK YO!

UM... THIS IS A PHOTO OF ME...
...WITH A MOUSTACHE DRAWN IN FELT TIP
S'NOT THAT I WANT ONE...

YE... ES. MOST OF YOU HAVE PRETTY MUCH GOT THE IDEA...
ANYONE ELSE?
LOU?

AHEM... I'VE WRITTEN A LITTLE ONE-ACT SURREALIST PLAY...
IT'S CALLED "DOUBTS"
I'VE ALSO MADE THE COSTUME...

HIPPOPOTAMUS!!!

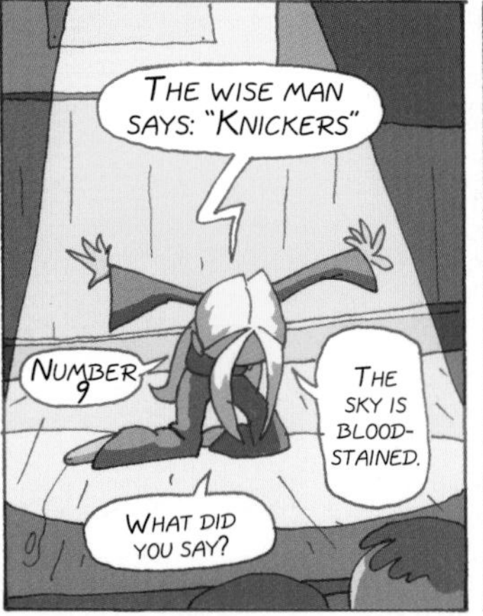
THE WISE MAN SAYS: "KNICKERS"
NUMBER 9
THE SKY IS BLOOD-STAINED.
WHAT DID YOU SAY?

WHERE IS HE? MY NAILS ARE COMING OFF!
SYMBIOSIS EQUINOX I AM... A WOMAN! EQUINOX I AM... A WOMAN!
THE SEA IS RAGING...
I... AAAAGH!

PARADOX AND SOLSTICE: I DIE AND I AM REBORN

THAT'S ODD: FOR ART, THERE'S NO GRADE, JUST THE ADDRESS OF A YOUTH PSYCHIATRIST.
GREAT ARTISTS ARE ALWAYS MISUNDERSTOOD.

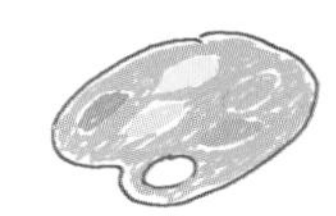

HI GIRLS!
3
LOOK, THERE'S YOUR ROMEO.
SSSH!

I'M HAVING A PARTY ON SATURDAY TO CELEBRATE THE END OF TERM AND MY BIRTHDAY. WILL YOU COME?
NO PROBLEM.
SURE.

GREAT. COOL THEN. GOTTA GO, LAST HISTORY LESSON OF THE YEAR!
'BYE
AAAAGH, PANIC...

PANIC? ARE YOU MAD! THIS PARTY'S THE PERFECT OPPORTUNITY FOR YOU TO DECLARE YOUR FEELINGS!
I'LL NEVER HAVE THE GUTS!
TOC! TOC!

WELL THINK! GIVE HIM A PRESENT THAT WILL SHOW HIM HOW YOU FEEL...
HUH... I'M TOTALLY BROKE, HARDLY ENOUGH TO BUY HIM A CD.
OH VERY ORIGINAL...

UNLESS... I KNOW! I'LL DO A PAINTING MYSELF IN WHICH I EXPRESS ALL MY FEELINGS FOR HIM: LOVE, ARDOUR, PASSION...
NOW THAT'S A GOOD IDEA!

RIGHT:
LOVE...

ARDOUR...
PASSION...
HAN! HAN!
SHLICHT!

MY MASTERPIECE ...
?

YERK!

AN ANCHOVY PIZZA? A SKIN DISEASE?
ANYWAY, IT'S UM... ORIGINAL...

OH, A CD, THANKS. CAN YOU PUT IT WITH THE OTHERS?

I PROMISE YOU, GOING TO SEE A PSYCHIATRIST DOESN'T MEAN YOU'RE MAD! IT MIGHT JUST HELP YOU IDENTIFY AND RESOLVE YOUR PROBLEMS... BESIDES, SOMETIMES IT'S GOOD TO BE ABLE TO TALK TO SOMEONE...

BACK OFF, OK?!

I'LL GO THIS ONCE, JUST TO MAKE YOU HAPPY!
THEN YOU'LL LEAVE ME IN PEACE!

BUMMER!
EVEN MY MOTHER THINKS I'M CRAZY! THAT'S ALL I NEED!!

51 SIGMUND FREUD STREET. HERE WE ARE...
51
DOCTOR FINKERSTEIN. JUST READING THE NAME MAKES YOU THINK OF A STRAITJACKET...

I CAN JUST SEE HIM, A BEARDED OLD FUDDY-DUDDY WHO'LL ASK YOU TO TELL HIM ABOUT YOUR DREAMS...
UH!UH! IF I TELL HIM HE'LL HAVE ME LOCKED UP STRAIGHT AWAY!

YOU MUST BE LOU. HI! I'M DOCTOR FINKERSTEIN!
?

SO YOU'VE BROUGHT YOUR FRIEND? OF COURSE, PEOPLE ARE USUALLY AFRAID OF SHRINKS!
HA! HA! I BET YOU THOUGHT I WAS A BEARDED OLD MAN!
UM... I'LL WAIT HERE.

SEE YOU NEXT WEEK, DOCTOR!
TAKE CARE!
?

WELL? YOU HAVEN'T SAID A WORD FOR TEN MINUTES... HOW WAS IT?

YOU KNOW WHAT? YOU SHOULD TRY IT... IT'S GOT NOTHING TO DO WITH NUTTERS. YOU TALK TO HER, AND YOU TALK TO HER, AND YOU UNDERSTAND LOADS OF STUFF ABOUT YOURSELF. HEY, I BET IT WOULD HELP YOU TO CHANNEL YOUR ENERGY AND DISCOVER...
BACK OFF! ALL RIGHT?

RIGHT. HERE GOES. I'M GOING TO DROP IN AND SAY HI TO TRISTAN.

TRISTAN? I THINK HE'S UP ON THE ROOF. YOU CAN GO UP, I'M SURE HE'LL BE DELIGHTED TO SEE YOU.

Blong Blong Bling Bling
I'M TOTALLY IN LOVE...

WOW, THAT'S AMAZING. I WISH I COULD PLAY THE GUITAR.
Bling Blong Blong
HEE! HEE! THAT WAS JUST A FEW BASIC CHORDS!

IF YOU LIKE, I CAN TEACH YOU! I'LL SHOW YOU A REALLY SIMPLE CHORD!
OH, DO YOU THINK I'LL BE ABLE TO?

PUT YOUR INDEX FINGER ON THE SECOND FRET OF THE THIRD STRING AND YOUR MIDDLE FINGER ON THE THIRD FRET OF THE SECOND STRING...
HOLD ON! HOLD ON!

BLONK!
OUCH!

NO! NO! THIS FINGER, THERE, AND UM... RELAX YOUR ARM....
AND...

UM... ER! YES... RIGHT, THAT'S IT. THAT SHOULD BE OK. NOW TRY!
TRY WHAT? OH, YES, THE GUITAR.
WELL?
Blong

Blong Blong Blong Blong!
THAT'S IT! YOU'VE GOT IT!

BLONK!
OH DRAT...
WILL YOU SHOW ME AGAIN?
Julien Neel 2003

KNOCK! KNOCK!
?

OH RICHARD, HI!
UM. HELLO, I...
I'M OFF TO WORK AS A SUMMER CAMP LEADER DURING THE HOLIDAYS AND I DROPPED IN TO SAY GOODBYE ...

OH YOU'RE OFF TO W...
YES, FOR TWO MONTHS
OK, UM... SEE YOU IN SEPTEMBER THEN?
YES, SEE YOU IN SEPTEMBER.
LOU'S OUT. THAT'S A PITY.
SAY BYE FOR ME...

TWO MONTHS

TWO MONTHS!

HEY, RICHARD, WAIT! I UM... I'LL COME TO THE STATION WITH YOU, I... UM... I'VE GOT TO GO TO THE SHOPS AND...

RIGHT, WELL...
YES, RIGHT, I...
SO, SEE YOU...
YES, AND TAKE CARE.
I
MY TRAIN'S...
YES, SEE Y...

AAAAGH... WHAT ON EARTH'S WRONG WITH ME? WHY DIDN'T I FLING MY ARMS AROUND HIM? AND WHY HAVEN'T I BEEN ABLE TO TELL HIM THAT...

AAAAGH... WHAT'S THE MATTER WITH ME? I SHOULD HAVE THROWN MY ARMS AROUND HER, KISSED HER AND TOLD HER THAT...

... AND THAT'S ALL?

UM... YES... WE PLAYED THE GUITAR ALL EVENING... IT WAS AMAZING AND...
BUT YOU DIDN'T TELL HIM YOU FANCIED HIM?
OH... UM... NO. I...

AAAAGH! I DON'T BELIEVE IT! YOU'RE AS BAD AS EACH OTHER! MADLY IN LOVE AND CAN'T GET IT TOGETHER TO MAKE THE FIRST MOVE! YOU KNOW WHAT.... YOU'RE AS BAD AS RICHARD AND YOUR MUM...
IF YOU DON'T DO SOMETHING YOU'LL END UP AS SAD OLD SPINSTERS! JUST IMAGINE!
?

I CAN JUST SEE IT. SCARY...
RIGHT. NOW GO ACROSS THE STREET AND LET YOUR HEART SPEAK!

RIGHT, THIS TIME I'M GONNA DO IT...

MY HEART'S BURSTING....
DONG!
DING!
BODOM BODOM BODOM

?

N... NOBODY IN...
WEIRD, THE DOOR'S HALF OPEN...

SHALL I?

¡¡¡¡¡¡K!

Thank you to Bruno, for... everything! Thank you to my family and to the three tricksters.

Oh yes! Now we've got a CAT
Chat
I'm hungry
Excuse my French
He arrived out of the blue one day through the window. He's squatted in our flat ever since. Cheek!
UNE JOURNÉE DU CHAT:
ZZZ 8h
ZZZ 14h
SCOFF SCOFF 17h
ZZZ 20h
He's sooo cute
He hasn't really got a name. Well, he has, but it changes all the time.
Some cats' names:
- CHACHOUMOU
- TIRE-AU-FLAN
- LA FLAQUE
- SUPERSATORI
- HULK
- MONGO ELVIS
- BOULET
- KID GERARD
- BRANDON VIII
Most of the time he looks grumpy as if to say:
I despise you
Give me cat food
R.
NOW
Sometimes he drives us nuts
AT THE BEGINNING OF THE YEAR A NEW NEIGHBOUR MOVED INTO OUR BUILDING
RiCHArd
R + M = ♥
HIHI
PFFF...
Richard's really cool. We soon made friends with him... especially mum...
HIM
Richard's only flaw is his jacket made from the skin of a dead sheep
ARGH! (what the poor creature)
When there's a full moon you can hear it bleat.
BÊÊÊ
It gives you the creeps
Richard's cool. He looks kind of grotty but he's really nice
Tee Hee!
Richard plays a giant violin for hours and Mum thinks that's amazing
I suspect Mum and Richard are madly in love with each other but they're dumb to realize it.
It's obvious, they're in love